D0378837

© 2002 by Barbour Publishing, Inc.

ISBN 1-58660-449-X

Cover art © EyeWire

Published by Barbour Books, an imprint of Barbour Publishing, Inc., P.O. Box 719, Uhrichsville, Ohio 44683, www.barbourbooks.com

Member of the
Evangelical Christian
Publishers Association

Printed in China.
5 4 3 2 1

Wise Men Still Seek Him Today

ELLYN SANNA
with VIOLA RUELKE GOMMER

When they saw the star,
they were overjoyed. . . .
They saw the child
with his mother Mary,
and they bowed down and worshiped him.
Then they opened their treasures
and presented him with gifts. . . .

MATTHEW 2:10–11

4

Contents

At this special time of the year,
may you share the wisdom
the wise men knew so long ago. . .
may you sense the presence
of the Christ Child in your life.

I

Wisdom

We all need wisdom. . .
Wisdom to choose the right paths to take in life. . .
Wisdom to know right from wrong. . .
Wisdom to see what truly matters most.
The wise men were willing to give up their homes,
their familiar habits,
and travel far to seek wisdom.
It takes courage to set out looking for something new.
But if we make this journey,
God will shine His light into our lives,
like the glimmer of that long-ago star.
All we have to do is follow.

And by the light of that same star,
Three wise men came from country far;
To seek for a king was their intent,
And to follow the star wherever it went.

This star drew nigh to the northwest,
O'er Bethlehem it took its rest;
And there it did both stop and stay,
Right over the place where Jesus lay.

"THE FIRST NOEL,"
Traditional Carol

*What was it that
made the wise men wise?
What wisdom did they demonstrate?*

The wise men noticed the sign that pointed them to Christ.
They were not too preoccupied with their own busy lives
to see that which no one else even noticed.

*Show me, Lord, where Your light glimmers in my life. Help me not be
so rushed that I hurry past, never noticing the signs of Your coming.*

When the wise men saw the star that pointed them to Christ, they committed their lives to discovering more. They could have talked and wondered about that star their whole lives, without ever knowing anything more about it—but instead, they allowed it to change the shape of how they lived. No longer rich, pampered kings, they became travelers, pilgrims into the unknown.

Give me strength, Lord, to follow You. . .even when I don't know where I'm going. When the way is dark and long, may I still follow Your light.

The Kings from the East

"Dear children," they asked in every town,
Three kings from the land of the sun,
"Which is the road to Bethlehem?"
But neither the old nor the young
Could tell, so the kings rode on:
Their guide was a golden star,
Which glittered ahead of them, high in the air,
So clear, so very clear.

The star stood still over Joseph's house,
They all of them stepped in:
The good ox lowed and the little child cried,
And the kings began to sing.

HEINRICH HEINE

True wisdom—
heaven's wisdom—
is found in unexpected places. . .
and makes us sing.

During the Second World War, Lieutenant Frank was a navigator aboard a plane. After a bombing raid, he noticed something was wrong and informed the pilot that the plane was moving into hostile territory. The pilot argued with Frank, pointing to the plane's "homing device," which indicated that they were right on course.

Frustrated, Frank told the pilot to look out the window. "What do you see?"

The pilot peered out into the dark night. "I don't see anything but stars."

"Yes," Frank responded, "and those stars tell me we're headed into enemy territory."

Convinced at last, the pilot turned the aircraft around and headed back to safety.

In what direction is your life heading? What are you using to guide you on your way? The wise men followed the star to Emmanuel, God-with-us. They were wise enough to follow the signs from heaven that led them to their hearts' desires.

Our world no longer follows stars. But those who are truly wise are still open to light from another realm, to wisdom that contradicts earth's common sense.

May your way be lit by stars. . .and may you, too, find your heart's desire.

A Prayer for True Wisdom
(George Washington's Prayer at Valley Forge)

Almighty God, Father of all,
to Thee we raise thankful hearts for
deliverance from the forces of evil.
Deliver us also, we beseech Thee,
from the greatest danger of ourselves.
Have mercy on us and forgive us for
our past in the present desolation of the world.
Awake us each time to a sense of our responsibility
in saving the world from ruin.
Open our minds and eyes and hearts to
the desperate plight of millions.
Arouse us from indifference into action.
Let none of us fail to give his utmost in sympathy,
understanding, thought, and effort.
Fulfill in us and through us Thy glorious intention that
Thy peace, Thy love, and Thy justice
may enter into the regeneration of the world.
Amen.

May God's wisdom light your life.

II

The Presence of
the Christ Child

Sometimes the Christ Child seems completely absent from our world. Innocence, love, and joy are sadly missing. We cannot even find Him in our own hearts.

But He is there. Sin hides Him from our sight. . .but the sun still shines behind the clouds, and Christ is always present in our lives.

I pray that you will see Him this Christmas season.

May Emmanuel find welcome
in our hearts,
Take flesh in our lives,
And be for all peoples
the welcome advent
Of redemption and grace.

THE ROMAN MISSAL

Though He be Lord of all,
The Christ Child is but very small.
Kneel then, and at His cradle lay,
Most gentle love this Christmas Day.

ANONYMOUS, 14TH CENTURY

Our minds on life's looming problems,
like bills and household chores,
job deadlines and doctor's appointments,
family quarrels and the latest diet,
we sometime forget to notice
that God's presence has crept
quietly and sweetly
into the smallest details of our lives,
like the sun on our face,
a warm hand in ours,
a child's laughter,
and a family's love.
This Christmas season, may you see
the Christmas Baby
at the heart
of your life.

*For me to be a saint is to be myself.
Therefore the problem of
sanctity and salvation
is in fact the problem of
finding out who I am
and discovering my true self.*

THOMAS MERTON

When we find our truest, deepest selves, we find God. And when we find God's presence, we find our true selves.

Isn't that what Christmas is all about?

Wise Men Still Seek Him Today

"You will seek me and find me when
you seek me with all your heart.
I will be found by you," declares the LORD.

JEREMIAH 29:13

"So I say to you:
Ask and it will be given to you;
seek and you will find;
knock and the door will be opened to you.
For everyone who asks receives;
he who seeks finds;
and to him who knocks,
the door will be opened."

LUKE 11:9–10

Sometimes we want to give up.
God doesn't seem to answer His door.
We're tired of searching for His face.
The Christmas story seems too good to be true,
a fairy tale meant for children.

But when Jesus comes,
He makes even tired, grown-up hearts
young again.
May you feel Him touch your heart
this Christmas season
and all year long.

III

Gifts

The Wise Men's Gifts

They brought the very best of what they had. . .
- Gold: the king of metals and the metal of kings.
- Frankincense: the scent of meditation and worship.
- Myrrh: a precious, perfumed ointment.

What can we bring the Christ Child?
- We can bestow on Him our gold. . .the riches of our life's blessings.
- We can give Him frankincense. . .our meditation and worship.
- We can offer Him myrrh. . .the sweet perfume of our talents and love.

He has given us so much.
How can we hold back when we give to Him?

Protect us, Lord, from stingy hearts.
May we give to You all we have.
Help us to build Your Kingdom
by sharing with others
the gifts You have so freely
given us.

AMEN.

A missionary was working with children in a poverty-stricken town. As she shared the story of Christ's birth, each child was given materials to make a small nativity scene. The shepherds, wise men, Mary, Joseph, animals, and Baby Jesus were all to be cut from cardboard and put into a crèche.

As the missionary looked over the children's work, she noticed that one boy had placed two babies in the manger. "What's this?" she asked him.

"Well," he said, "one baby is Jesus, and the other one is me." He looked up at his teacher. "The wise men gave the baby presents—but I don't have anything to give Him. So I thought I'd lie beside Him and keep Him warm."

What gift will you give?

Your love. . .

Your warmth. . .

Your self?

Those are the best gifts—the gifts the Christ Child treasures most of all.

A Question

One of the perennial questions asked at Christmas is: "What do you want for Christmas?"

What is on your Christmas list this year?

_____

_____

_____

_____

_____

_____

_____

_____

You may have listed jewelry, clothing, games, money, a trip, books, CDs, videos. . . Did you include time with dear friends, the ability to give to others in need, increased love for God and others? What is your deepest heart's desire for Christmas this year? If you could ask God for anything, anything at all, what would you ask? Make sure you add that secret heart-treasure to your list.

Another Question

What is God's desire for you at Christmas this year? What does He most wish you would give Him? (Consider: Does He want more time from you. . .more money. . .more worship. . .more willingness to be of service to others?) If Jesus could make a Christmas list, what do you think would be on it?

_____

_____

_____

_____

_____

_____

_____

_____

_____

_____

_____

_____

Here are some gift ideas for that most important person in your life—God.

- A thoughtful note to someone who is alone.
- A call to someone with whom you haven't spoken for a long time.
- A homemade gift hand-delivered to a neighbor.
- A word of encouragement for someone who is downhearted.
- Forgiveness for someone who has hurt you.
- A hug for someone who feels unloved.
- A grocery store certificate to a family in need.
- A smile for a complete stranger.
- A kind word for the next angry person you encounter.

You are the gift.
Your presence is embodied in each action. . .and so is God's.
Offer God's love to those around you.

IV

A Christmas Prayer

During this Christmas season, I'm praying this prayer that's rooted in the Scriptures:

May gifts from God
gladden your way. . .

Every good and perfect gift is from above,
coming down from the Father of the heavenly lights,
who does not change like shifting shadows.

JAMES 1:17

And bring you the peace of
this glorious day. . .

"Glory to God in the highest,
and on earth peace to men."

LUKE 2:14

Joy for each sorrow. . .

But the angel said to them,
"Do not be afraid.
I bring you good news of great joy
that will be for all the people."

LUKE 2:10

Cheer for each ill. . .

God is our refuge and strength,
an ever-present help in trouble.

PSALM 46:1

Hope for tomorrow. . .

Set your hope fully on the grace to be given you when Jesus Christ is revealed.

1 PETER 1:13

Faith in His will. . .

"Have faith in God," Jesus answered.
"I tell you the truth, if anyone says to this mountain,
'Go, throw yourself into the sea,'
and does not doubt in his heart. . .
it will be done for him."

MARK 11:22–23

Blessings from heaven
in all that you do.

*A faithful man
will be richly blessed.*

PROVERBS 28:20

*I constantly remember you
in my prayers.*

2 TIMOTHY 1:3

Merry Christmas!
May you seek God's wisdom
and know His presence during the new year to come.
I will keep you in my prayers.